Make a New Friend in Je

PassAlong Arch® Books help you
Jesus with friends close to you and
children all around the world!

When you've enjoyed this story, pass it
along to a friend. When your friend is fin-
ished, mail this book to the address below. Concordia Gospel
Outreach promises to deliver your book to a boy or girl some-
where in the world to help him or her learn about Jesus.

Myself

My name _____

My address _____

_____

My PassAlong Friend

My name _____

My address _____

When you're ready to give
your PassAlong Arch® Book to a
new friend who doesn't know
about Jesus, mail it to

Concordia Gospel Outreach
3547 Indiana Avenue
St. Louis, MO 63118

PassAlong Series

God's Good Creation
Noah's Floating Zoo
Baby Moses' River Ride
Moses and the Freedom Flight
Jonah's Fishy Adventure
Daniel in the Dangerous Den
Baby Jesus, Prince of Peace
Jesus Stills the Storm
Jesus and Jairus' Little Girl
Jesus' Big Picnic
God's Easter Plan
Peter and the Biggest Birthday

Copyright © 1995 Concordia Publishing House
3558 S. Jefferson Avenue, St. Louis, MO 63118-3968
Manufactured in the United States of America

1 2 3 4 5 6 7 8 9 10   04 03 02 01 00 99 98 97 96 95

Moses and the Freedom Flight

Exodus 2:11–15:21 for Children

Carol Greene
Illustrated by Michelle Dorenkamp

CPH™

SAINT LOUIS

oses grew up strong and tall in
      Egyptland,
And still he wondered what God
      planned.
"When I was a baby, He took care of me.
But why I'm here, I just don't see."

Then a cruel Egyptian hurt a Hebrew
      slave,
And Moses sent him to his grave.
That was that, he knew he had to run
      away.
So off he dashed that very day.

"Run, Moses, run!"

He ended up in Midian. He found a wife,
And there he led a shepherd's life.
One day he was shepherding and saw
    a sight—
A green bush burning clear and bright.

But it didn't burn away, and Moses
    thought,
"That fire's not acting as it ought."
While he still was thinking, "How
    extremely odd!"
A voice said, "Moses, this is God.

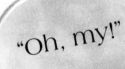

"Oh, my!"

Don't come any closer. This is holy
    ground."
Moses couldn't make a sound.
God said, "Pharaoh makes my people
    suffer. So
You tell him, 'Let My people go!'

"I'm bringing them to Canaan, where
    they'll all live free."
Moses gulped and squeaked,
    "Who? Me?
Who am I to try that mighty deed to do?"
God said, "I will go with you."

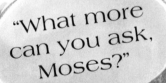

"What more
can you ask,
Moses?"

M oses kept protesting, but of course,
    God won.
His plan for Moses had begun.
"Let your brother, Aaron, help you,"
    God said. "Go!"
Moses went, his head bowed low.

Back in Egypt, Moses and his brother
    told
God's people of God's plan so bold.
Then they went to Pharaoh, and with
    eyes aglow
Said, "God says, 'Let My people go!'"

"Brave Moses! Brave Aaron!"

Who is God?" said Pharaoh. "I don't think
I know.
And I won't let your people go.
Up till now I gave you straw to make
my bricks.
Now find your own to fix the mix."

That would be impossible, as Moses knew.
God's people cried, "What shall we do?"
"I will help," said God. "Now, Moses,
here's My plan."
The next day the first plague began.

"Watch out,
Pharaoh.
God has a
plan."

The brothers met with Pharaoh by the river
    Nile.
"You'll know our God," said Moses,
    while Aaron raised his staff.
The water turned to blood.
It was a nasty-smelling flood.

Pharaoh's heart was hard. He simply
    turned his head.
"I still won't let you go," he said.
Seven days dragged by till Moses went again.
"You can't go!" Pharaoh said. And then . . .

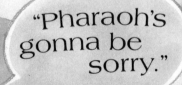

"Pharaoh's gonna be sorry."

As God ordered, brother Aaron raised his hand.

At once frogs covered Egyptland.

Hopping through the houses, crawling up the folk,

Those frogs took over. Croak, croak, croak!

Pharaoh went to dinner. Frogs sat in his bowls.

They trailed slime on his royal scrolls.

When he took a bath, they flopped on Pharaoh's head,

And plopped in piles on Pharaoh's bed.

"Yuck!"

You can go," cried Pharaoh, "if you'll just
        suppress
This hopping, flopping, plopping mess!"
When the frogs were gone, though,
        Pharaoh shook his head.
"I changed my mind. You'll stay," he said.

Then God turned the dust of Egypt into gnats.
They swarmed on mats and hats and cats.
They covered people's bodies, and they
        stung and bit.
But Pharaoh said, "You'll stay. That's it!"

"I do not like gnats!"

Time and time again the brothers said,
"You know,
God says, 'Let My people go!'"
Pharaoh would say, "Yes," until the plague
had passed,
Then change his mind right at the last.

Clouds of flies struck Egypt. Then the cattle
died.
Boils hurt people till they cried.
Hail flattened crops, and locusts ate the food.
Thick darkness fell. It did no good.

"Pharaoh's heart must be hard as a brick!"

Moses told God's people, "Come, the time
is near.
You'll eat a special dinner here,
Paint lamb's blood on your doorframes,
and then you'll see,
God means to set His people free."

Midnight came, and the firstborn
Egyptians died.
God's people waited, safe inside.
Pharaoh saw his own dead son, and
that's when he
Cried, "Moses, go! And please bless me."

"At last!"

Out of Egypt poured God's people, free at
    last.
Four hundred thirty years had passed
Since they'd come and ended up as
    Pharaoh's slaves.
Now Egypt marveled, "Their God saves!"

Children, men, women, and their cattle fled
Into the desert. At their head
Moved a fiery pillar to show the way
At night—a cloudy one by day.

"What a parade!"

Back in Egypt, fickle Pharaoh changed his
    mind.
"Call out the army! We will find
Those people in the desert, and we'll bring
    them back."
And so he set off on their track.

Then God's people wound up in an awful
    bind,
As Pharaoh's army marched behind,
While before them stretched the Red Sea,
    deep and blue.
"It's your fault, Moses. We blame you!"

"I'm sure
God has
something
planned."

Moses, though, had talked with God and
    raised his hand.
It happened just as God had planned.
Swish! The waters parted. Dry land lay
    below.
"Stop crabbing," Moses said, "and go."

Water to the left of them and to the right,
God's people marched, a wondrous sight.
But when Pharaoh's armies tried that
    same dry ground,
The water crashed, and they all drowned.

"Good-bye,
Pharaoh!"

Moses and God's people sang a song of
praise.
"My God will guide me all my days.
He is my salvation. He has rescued me,
Drowned Pharaoh's army in the sea."

Moses' sister Miriam took up the song.
The other women danced along.
"God is our salvation. He will always be.
Sing praise to God. He set us free!"

"Now that's a good song."

You can join that joyful song beside the sea.
With His own Son, God set you free,
Free to follow where He guides for all your
    days.
So sing it out—your song of praise.

"God sent Jesus to set you free. So sing!"

SADIQ

and the
Fun Run

BY SIMAN NUURALI

ART BY ANJAN SARKAR

PICTURE WINDOW BOOKS
a capstone imprint

Sadiq is published by Picture Window Books,
a Capstone imprint
1710 Roe Crest Drive
North Mankato, Minnesota 56003
www.mycapstone.com

Copyright © 2020 Capstone

Library of Congress Cataloging-in-Publication Data
Names: Nuurali, Siman, author. | Sarkar, Anjan, illustrator.
Title: Sadiq and the fun run / by Siman Nuurali ; illustrated by Anjan Sarkar.
Description: North Mankato, Minnesota : Picture Window Books, [2019] |
    Series: Sadiq | Summary: Eight-year-old Sadiq wants to try out for the
    youth football team like his friends, but his parents feel he is too
    young, and instead suggest that he take up running and join the track
    club—Sadiq feels that running is wimpy, but the coach convinces him that
    running races can be fun as well.
Identifiers: LCCN 2018052127 | ISBN 9781515838814 (hardcover) | ISBN
    9781515845669 (pbk.) | ISBN 9781515838852 (ebook pdf)
Subjects: LCSH: Running—Juvenile fiction. | Running races—Juvenile fiction.
    | Muslim families—Juvenile fiction. | Children of immigrants—Juvenile
    fiction. | Africans—United States—Juvenile fiction. |
    Friendship—Juvenile fiction. | CYAC: Running—Fiction. | Racing—Fiction.
    | Muslims—United States—Fiction. | Immigrants—Fiction. |
    Africans—United States—Fiction. | Friendship—Fiction.
Classification: LCC PZ7.1.N9 Saf 2019 | DDC [Fic]—dc23
LC record available at https://lccn.loc.gov/2018052127

Design by Brann Garvey
Design Element: Shutterstock/Irtsya

Printed and bound in China.
1671

TABLE OF
CONTENTS

FACTS ABOUT SOMALIA

- Most Somali people belong to one of four major groups: the Darod, Isaaq, Hawiye, and Dir.
- Many Somalis are nomadic. That means they travel from place to place. They search for water, food, and land for their animals.
- Somalia is mostly desert. It doesn't rain often there.
- The camel is an important animal to Somali people. Camels can survive a long time without food or water.
- Around ninety-nine percent of all Somalis are Muslim.

SOMALI TERMS

baba (BAH-baah)—a common word for father

cambuulo (UHM-boo-loh)—a dish made up of rice and beans, with sesame oil and sugar drizzled on top

hooyo (HOY-yoh)—mother

salaam (sa-LAHM)—a short form of Arabic greeting, used by many Muslims. It also means "peace."

wiilkeyga (wil-KAY-gaah)—my son

CHAPTER 1

FOOTBALL TRYOUTS

On Sunday afternoon, Sadiq went
to the park near his house. Leaves
crunched under his feet as he walked.
He spotted Zaza and Manny tossing a
football back and forth on the field.

"Sadiq!" called Zaza. "Come join
us! We're practicing for football tryouts
tomorrow."

Manny tossed the football to Sadiq
as he walked closer. "Are you guys both
going to try out?" asked Sadiq.

"I am," replied Zaza. "Both of my older brothers play football. It looks like so much fun."

"Me too!" said Manny. "I hope I get on the team. The uniforms are so cool!"

"Are you trying out, Sadiq?" asked Zaza.

"I would like to, but I'll have to ask my parents first," said Sadiq.

The boys continued to pass the football to each other. They practiced snapping the football. They practiced short throws and long throws. And finally, they practiced catching the ball while running. *Zaza and Manny are really good!* Sadiq thought. *Maybe if I practice enough I'll be just as good.*

When it started to get dark outside, Sadiq headed home. Right away he went to look for his mom. He wanted to talk to her about joining the football team. Zaza and Manny had made it sound so exciting!

"*Salaam,* Hooyo!" Sadiq called as he pushed through the front door. It smelled of *cambuulo,* a bean dish made with butter and sugar. It was one of Sadiq's favorite meals, and he was hungry!

"Salaam, Sadiq," Hooyo said. She looked up from a magazine she was reading while dinner cooked on the stovetop beside her. "How was the park?"

"Good! Zaza, Manny, and I played football," Sadiq explained. "Tryouts for the team are tomorrow. Is Baba home? I wanted to ask you both if I could join."

"Aren't you all too young to play football?" said Hooyo. She looked a little worried.

"What's this about football?"
Baba asked as he walked into the
kitchen.

"Pull up a chair for your baba and
set the table, please," Hooyo said as
she passed some plates and utensils to
Sadiq.

"I want to try out for the school
team," Sadiq said.

"I don't think that's a good idea.
You're only eight, *wiilkeyga,*" Baba
said, sitting down. "Your brother
didn't start playing until he was
twelve."

"I agree," said Hooyo. She pulled
some napkins out of a drawer and
handed them to Sadiq.

Sadiq went around the table and put a napkin at each place setting as he complained. "But Zaza and Manny are going to try out! Their parents don't think they're too young."

"That may be true, wiilkeyga, but football can be a very rough game. I don't want you to get hurt," said Baba.

"I would be very worried too," said Hooyo. "I think you should wait until you're older, like your brother."

Sadiq looked down at the floor, disappointed.

"I know you're sad, Sadiq, but is there another club you can join at school? Something other than football?" asked Hooyo.

Sadiq shook his head sadly. "There's no school soccer team," he said, "and I want to be on a team with Manny and Zaza."

Baba spoke up. "We got your school newsletter the other day. There's going to be a running club starting later this week, and there aren't any tryouts! Ahmed Bilaal is coaching it."

"Is he the runner who qualified for the national team?" asked Hooyo.

"Yes!" said Baba. "A famous runner will be coaching at your school, Sadiq."

"But what about my friends? Zaza and Manny are going to have so much fun without me," Sadiq said.

"They'll still be your friends, wiilkeyga," Hooyo said. "Maybe you can take them running with you."

Just then, Sadiq's brother, Nuurali, wandered into the room. "Running will help you get better at soccer," he said. "It helps me stay in shape for football. That's why I run a few times a week."

Sadiq perked up. He was still disappointed about football, but he did *love* soccer. "I guess I can give it a try," he said.

* * *

"My parents won't let me try out for football," said Sadiq as he, Zaza, and Manny waited for the bus to pick them up on Monday morning.

"Why not?" Manny said.

"They think I'm too young. Nuurali didn't start playing until he was twelve," Sadiq explained.

"Did you tell them that we're both doing it?" asked Zaza. He sounded very disappointed.

Sadiq nodded. "They want me to try the Running Club instead."

"Running?!" Manny said. "Running is so boring."

"I hoped we'd all be on the team together," said Zaza.

"I know," said Sadiq as the bus pulled up. "Me too."

CHAPTER 2

SUPER RACER

After school on Tuesday, Sadiq walked to the bus alone. He felt sorry for himself. Manny and Zaza had made the football team. They'd found out at lunchtime, and today was their first practice.

As he walked past the football field, Sadiq could see his friends warming up. He felt left out. Manny and Zaza looked really tough in their football gear.

As Sadiq watched, a player wearing a blue jersey ran with the ball. Players wearing yellow jerseys chased him down the field. They caught up and tackled him! The player who had been running with the ball got up and dusted himself off. He jogged back to his teammates.

I don't understand why Baba and Hooyo won't let me play football, Sadiq thought. *I could become strong like that player. It would be so much fun to tackle people!*

When Sadiq got home, he was not in a good mood. He was upset after seeing how much fun Zaza, Manny, and all the other kids were having.

He went straight to his room, where he found Nuurali doing homework on the computer they shared for schoolwork.

Sadiq threw his backpack on the floor and flopped facedown on his bed.

"What's the matter, Sadiq?" asked Nuurali. "Are you all right?"

"No!" said Sadiq, his voice muffled in his pillow. He looked up. "I saw Zaza and Manny playing football. They were having all the fun in the world! It's not fair that Baba and Hooyo won't let me play."

"Well you could have fun in your Running Club pretty soon," said Nuurali. "Don't you start practice tomorrow?"

"Yes, practice starts tomorrow. But I'd rather be at football practice," said Sadiq as he sat up and faced his brother.

"You won't know until you try," said Nuurali. "I could use a break from my homework. Would you like to come running with me? It might help you get ready for your first practice."

"No," said Sadiq, sulking.

"Come on, Sadiq," Nuurali said. "I don't want to run alone!"

"Fine," said Sadiq. He got up and dragged himself to the closet to find his soccer clothes and tennis shoes.

After Nuurali and Sadiq got changed, they met up by the front door.

"My football coach says to always start with a slow jog. It helps you save energy so you don't get tired right away," Nuurali said as he tied his shoelaces.

They went outside and started running down the block.

"You have to loosen your arms and keep them close to your body," said Nuurali.

After a few minutes, Sadiq started to feel hot and thirsty. "I don't really want to jog anymore, Nuurali," he said.

"We only just started, Sadiq," said Nuurali. "Let's at least get to the end of this block."

"But it's so far away," said Sadiq, slowing to a walk.

"Come on, Sadiq!" Nuurali called over his shoulder. "Breathe in and out. Before you know it, we'll be home!"

"I didn't want to go in the first place," said Sadiq. "I just came because you asked."

Nuurali slowed down so he could walk with Sadiq.

"You know, Sadiq," Nuurali said, "if you get really good at running you might even be able to compete in track and field or cross country when you're in middle school."

Sadiq was now dragging his feet along the pavement.

"Running will also help you get better at other sports like football and soccer," said Nuurali, smiling.

"I guess so," said Sadiq. He kicked a rock down the sidewalk.

"Come on, Super Racer!" Nuurali called. "Last one home does the dishes tonight!" He laughed as he started running again.

Sadiq sighed and ran after his brother.

CHAPTER 3

RUNNING CLUB

The next day, Sadiq went to the
track after school. It was time for the
first Running Club practice, and Sadiq
was nervous. Running with Nuurali
had been hard. *What if I'm not any
good at running?* Sadiq thought. A
young man wearing a tracksuit and
holding a clipboard was already on
the track when Sadiq arrived. There
were several kids surrounding him.

"Hello there!" the man said. "I'm
Ahmed. I'll be your running coach."
He held out his hand to Sadiq.

"I'm Sadiq." Sadiq shook Ahmed's hand.

When everyone had arrived, Ahmed told them, "The Running Club will meet after school for practice each day. Toward the end of the season, we'll all run in a 5K Fun Run. We will need to train properly so we don't get too tired or sore."

Next they went around the circle for introductions. Sadiq knew a couple of the kids who were in his grade. He had never met some of the others.

When they were done, Ahmed asked if they had any questions.

"Is it true you've won medals?" asked a boy named Hafid. "You must be fast."

Ahmed laughed. "I have won medals in some races," he said. "And I still hold the state's junior record for the fifteen-hundred meter track race."

"Wow!" said Sadiq.

"Was it hard training to compete?" asked Grace.

"It was," said Ahmed. "I used to wake up every morning at five. I would run for an hour before school. Sometimes I wanted to quit. But my baba encouraged me to keep training."

Five o'clock?! Sadiq thought. *It must take a lot of hard work to become such a fast runner.*

Next it was time to warm up. The team did jumping jacks and stretches.

"Bend over as far as you can and touch your toes," said Ahmed, leading them through some stretches. "You should have a slight bend in your knees."

"That's easy!" said Hafid.

But when Hafid tried to do it, he couldn't touch his toes. He lost his balance and fell forward onto the grass! "It's harder than I thought," he said, laughing.

After stretching, Ahmed explained their workout. "I would like you all to take two laps around the track. Jog at a pace that's comfortable for you."

They all took off.

A tall girl named Hayla ran beside Sadiq. "Hi!" she said, smiling. "My dad says I have long legs and that's good for running."

"I'm not very tall. I don't know if that's good or bad for running," said Sadiq, smiling back.

After one lap, Hafid piped up. "Let's race!"

Hafid, Hayla, and Sadiq all sprinted ahead of the group.

Soon they crossed the finish line, followed by the rest of the team. They were all breathing hard.

"So, team, how do you feel?" asked Ahmed.

"Ver–very tired. I didn't . . . thin–
think it was this . . . hard," said Sadiq,
out of breath.

"I'm exhausted," said Hayla.

"That was a good start," Ahmed
said. "But at our first practice, you
shouldn't be sprinting. You have to
learn to pace yourself. Can anyone tell
me what *pace* means?"

"It means to go at a steady speed—
not too fast or too slow," said a girl
named Kianna.

"Right!" said Ahmed. "You want to
make sure you can keep your pace for
the whole time you're running. It will
get easier as the season goes on."

"I don't . . . think so . . . ," said
Hafid, still breathing hard.

Ahmed laughed. "I promise, the first
day is the hardest."

Everyone was silent except for the
huffing and puffing.

"Let's all jog in place for a few
minutes to let our heart rates slow,"
said Ahmed. "It will help us breathe
better and help our bodies recover."

The kids did as they were told. After a few minutes Ahmed asked them to stop and take a water break.

"Does anyone have any questions?" asked Ahmed as everyone got their water bottles.

"How far are we going to run at practice?" a boy named Matt asked.

"Good question, Matt," said Ahmed. "It will be different every practice, but the most we will run is three miles. The Fun Run we'll participate in at the end of the season is about three miles also."

"The most I've ever run is one mile!" said Grace. "That was for soccer practice."

"If you play soccer, I bet you've run more than a mile!" said Ahmed. "Most soccer players run several miles during a game."

Sadiq was surprised by that. "I play soccer," he said excitedly to Hayla and Hafid. "I bet I can run three miles!"

"Me too," Hafid said.

"Next time let's work on our pace. Then we won't get so tired," said Hayla.

"Good work today, team!" said Ahmed. "Practice is over. I'll see you tomorrow."

CHAPTER 4

LEFT OUT

"How is football practice going?"
Sadiq asked Zaza and Manny at lunch
on Thursday.

"It is *awesome*!" said Manny,
grinning.

"I wish you had been there yesterday
to see our first scrimmage!" Zaza said.
He took a sip of his juice. "Manny
and I were on the same team. We
were down by three points with only
a minute left. The whole team was on
their feet cheering."

"Our quarterback, Jack, threw the ball way down the field to Eric," said Manny. "He was so far away we thought the ball would go out of bounds."

"But Eric jumped up really high and caught the ball," said Manny.

"He ran faster than I have ever seen anyone run and then . . . TOUCHDOWN!" said Zaza.

Sadiq nodded and said, "Cool," but he was feeling very left out. Zaza and Manny hadn't asked him anything about Running Club.

After a minute or two of silence, Sadiq spoke up. "Running Club is also pretty cool. Our coach is a famous athlete."

"What'd you do at practice?" Zaza
asked.

"We did stretching exercises and
then ran a couple of laps," said Sadiq.

"That's it?" said Zaza. He laughed,
looking at Manny.

"That doesn't sound super tough,"
said Manny.

"It was actually kind of difficult,"
Sadiq said quietly.

Why are they being so rude? Sadiq wondered. *Running is just as tough as football.*

Embarrassed, he packed up the rest of his lunch and went back to class early.

* * *

That afternoon at Running Club practice, Sadiq couldn't stop thinking about what Manny and Zaza had said. He felt annoyed and embarrassed that his friends didn't think running was a tough sport. Distracted, Sadiq slowed to a walk.

"What's wrong, buddy?" asked Ahmed, jogging up alongside him.

"Nothing," said Sadiq. He didn't really want to talk about it.

"You can talk to me if something's bothering you, Sadiq," said Ahmed. "I know that being unhappy can really affect your running."

"My friends bragged about how tough their football team is," said Sadiq. "It made me think running isn't as tough."

"In order to be a good football player, you have to be a really good runner as well."

"That's true," said Sadiq. That made him feel a little better.

"When I was a boy, I wanted to become a fast runner but I didn't want to train. Then one day at practice I stepped in a hole and twisted my ankle," said Ahmed.

"Ouch!" said Sadiq.

"I went from not wanting to run to not being able to walk very well. I had to use crutches for a couple of weeks and watch as my teammates competed," Ahmed explained.

"That doesn't sound fun," said Sadiq.

"It wasn't," said Ahmed. "But sitting out while the others had fun and improved made me appreciate running!"

Sadiq thought about that. If he wasn't able to run, he'd be sad too!

"From that day on," Ahmed said, "I was determined to practice as much as I could. Running became more fun. That is how I became a good runner."

"I'm sorry I wasn't trying today," said Sadiq. "I promise to try hard from now on."

"That's great," said Ahmed. "High five?" He held out his hand.

"High five!" said Sadiq. He slapped Ahmed's hand in return.

CHAPTER 5

THE FUN RUN

For the next few weeks, Sadiq worked
very hard with the rest of his team. He
was getting much better. Sadiq could
run many laps without stopping or
slowing down! He was starting to like
running, but he still missed his friends.

Manny and Zaza had tried to talk
to him a few times, but Sadiq was still
upset by what they'd said to him about
running. He didn't want to hang out
with his friends if they gave him a hard
time about running being an easy sport.

"Okay, team," Ahmed said after practice one day. "Next weekend is the Fun Run. Remember—it's not just about winning. But I want everyone to try their very best and finish feeling proud."

"Do you have any advice for us, Coach?" asked Hayla.

"It's a good idea to team up and run together in groups," said Ahmed. "That way you can push each other when one of you gets tired."

"Want to run together?" Hafid whispered to Hayla and Sadiq.

The trio nodded and smiled at one another.

* * *

Finally it was time for the Fun Run! Sadiq was very excited, but he was also nervous. His family drove him to the course, then went to find a spot to watch. There were tons of kids around, all in running gear! It took Sadiq a few minutes to spot his running team.

"Hi, you guys!" Sadiq called to them.

"Hi, Sadiq!" they all replied, waving at him.

"Gather 'round, kids. I have a surprise for you!" said Ahmed.

"What is it?" asked Hafid.

Ahmed leaned down and opened a box. He took out . . . UNIFORMS! They were silver, with all the kids' names printed in purple on the back.

"Look how cool they are!" said Sadiq.

"I love this lightning bolt on the front side," said Hayla.

"That's because we are fast like lightning!" said Hafid, laughing.

* * *

Soon it was time for the race. Ahmed gave the team a pep talk. "Remember to stay focused and try your best," he said. "And team up!"

Sadiq and his friends jogged over to the starting line and waited for the signal.

"Ready . . . set . . . go!" the starter yelled.

Sadiq, Hafid, and Hayla teamed up and took the lead right away. A few other runners ran just behind them. Sadiq set the pace, and Hafid and Hayla ran a step behind him. Soon they had finished one mile!

They were running too hard to say much to each other. Their pace was fast, but Sadiq felt like he could keep going.

Hafid kept pushing himself, but halfway through the second mile, he started to fade.

"I don't think I can keep up," said Hafid. He looked tired. "You should go ahead."

Sadiq could see Hayla was also falling behind, but he didn't want to leave his friends.

"I'll run with Hafid," said Hayla as they completed the second mile.

"Are you sure?" asked Sadiq.

"Yes," said Hayla. "We'll be right behind you."

"Okay, good luck!" Sadiq said as he took off. Sadiq pushed himself and ran faster than he had ever run before.

Running had seemed easier with Hayla and Hafid. He started to feel really tired.

Sadiq looked up to see how far he was from the finish line. Just then he spotted two familiar faces in the crowd.

Zaza and Manny! They had come to watch him race! *But how did they find out about the race?* Sadiq wondered.

He ran even harder, wanting to impress them. He wanted to show everyone how hard he had been working at practice. He pushed himself harder and harder until he crossed the finish line.

Sadiq had won!

His family ran down from the stands to congratulate him. Baba lifted him up in the air!

"Good job, Sadiq!" said Baba. "That was a really great run!"

Just then, Ahmed jogged over and gave Sadiq a high five.

"How did you run so fast?" asked Hooyo.

"I don't know!" said Sadiq. He was still breathing hard.

"He trained really well and worked very hard," replied Ahmed.

"We're very proud of you, Sadiq," Hooyo said.

Soon Hayla and Hafid crossed the finish line together. They had tied for second place! Before Sadiq could make it over to congratulate them, Zaza and Manny ran over to him. "Hi, champ!" said Zaza, hugging Sadiq.

"Hi, guys!" Sadiq said. He high-fived Manny. "How did you know my race was today?"

"We saw a sign in school," Manny said. "I can't believe how fast you ran!"

"So you don't think running is for wimps after all?" Sadiq asked. "You really hurt my feelings when you said that."

"We're really sorry we said running seemed easy," said Manny.

"We didn't mean to make you feel bad," said Zaza. "And it seems like running is really tough."

"It's okay. But you're right. Running *is* hard," said Sadiq.

"So what do you think, Sadiq?" asked Ahmed. "Will you stay in Running Club?"

"Yes!" Sadiq said. He turned to Zaza and Manny. "Do you want to come to Running Club sometime?" he asked.

"Can we?" asked Zaza excitedly, looking up at Ahmed.

"Of course you can," replied Ahmed. "We have one more practice this season. It's on Monday after school. Everyone is welcome."

"Football season is over now. Maybe we can come with you!" said Manny.

"I hope I'm not still tired from the race by then," said Sadiq.

Everyone laughed.

GLOSSARY

affect (uh-FEKT)—to influence or change someone or something

appreciate (uh-PREE-shee-ate)—to enjoy or value somebody or something

champ (CHAMP)—short for *champion*; the winner of a competition

compete (kuhm-PEET)—to try hard to outdo others at a task, race, or contest

congratulate (kuhn-GRACH-uh-late)— to offer good wishes to someone when something good has happened

impress (im-PRES)—to make someone feel admiration or respect

introduction (in-truh-DUHK-shuhn)— the presentation of one person to another

muffled (MUHF-uhld)—made a sound quieter or less clear

newsletter (NOOZ-let-ur)—a short written report that tells the recent news of an organization

pace (PASE)—a rate of speed, or to move at a certain speed

qualified (KWAH-luh-fide)—became eligible for a competition by reaching a certain standard

quarterback (KWOR-tur-bak)—in football, the player who leads the offense by throwing the ball or handing it to a runner

recover (ri-KUHV-ur)—to return to a normal state of health or strength

scrimmage (SKRIM-ij)—a practice game between two teams

tackle (TAK-uhl)—in football, knock or throw a player to the ground in order to stop the player from moving forward

touchdown (TUHCH-doun)—in football, a play in which the ball is carried over the opponent's goal line, scoring six points

wimp (WIMP)—a weak person

TALK ABOUT IT

1. What reasons did Sadiq's parents give for not letting him try out for football? Do you think they were being fair?

2. Sadiq feels left out when his friends Manny and Zaza talk about their football team. Share an experience you've had of feeling left out.

3. Sadiq receives a lot of encouragement as he trains for the Fun Run. Who helps Sadiq prepare? Discuss how they help him.

WRITE IT DOWN

1. Write an article for Sadiq's school newsletter about the Fun Run. You can interview Sadiq and others in the Running Club for your story.

2. Ahmed is famous for his running ability. Have you ever met someone famous? If so, write a paragraph explaining your experience. If not, write a paragraph about a famous person you would love to meet.

3. At first, running is not so easy for Sadiq. Have you ever tried something that was difficult at first? Write a paragraph about your experience.

HOME WORKOUT!

Sadiq learns to condition himself better when he joins the Running Club. With this short home workout, you can too! Make sure to pace yourself and take water breaks if you get tired. This workout can also be done with a partner.

WHAT YOU NEED:

- space to move around
- clothes suited for exercise
- tape
- water

WHAT TO DO:

1. Find a space in your home where you'll have plenty of room to move around.

2. Place a line of tape in your workout area. This will be used for one of the exercises.

3. Start your workout with stretches. It's important for your muscles to be stretched before any workout!

4. Do ten sit-ups. You may need a partner to help keep your feet on the ground.

5. Now complete ten push-ups.

6. Do fifteen jumping jacks.

7. Try to jump back and forth over the line of tape fifteen times.

8. Repeat the workout until you feel like you need a break. See if you can increase your numbers of sit-ups, push-ups, jumping jacks, and tape line jumps the more times you do the workout.

9. Make sure to drink water after your workout.

CREATORS

Siman Nuurali grew up in Kenya. She now lives in Minnesota. Siman and her family are Somali—just like Sadiq and his family! She and her five children love to play badminton and board games together. Siman works at Children's Hospital, and in her free time, she also enjoys writing and reading.

Anjan Sarkar is a British illustrator based in Sheffield, England. Since he was little, Anjan has always loved drawing stuff. And now he gets to draw stuff all day for his job. Hooray! In addition to the Sadiq series, Anjan has been drawing mischievous kids, undercover aliens, and majestic tigers for other exciting children's book projects.